Enduring Words

OF
LOVE
AND
COMFORT

Enduring Words

OF
LOVE
AND
COMFORT

The Five Mile Press

The Five Mile Press

The Five Mile Press Pty Ltd
950 Stud Road, Rowville
Victoria 3178
Australia

Email: publishing@fivemile.com.au
Website: www.fivemile.com.au

First published 2006

Compiled by Margaret Miller
Designed by Zoe Murphy

Printed in China

ISBN 1 74124 949 X

CONTENTS

PREFACE

From the euphoria of first love to the security of close friendship to the despair of love lost, this beautiful anthology of quotations reflects the joy, the trials, and the sorrow that accompany all forms of love and friendship.

The timeless passages, some more than 300 years old, testify to the unchanging nature of love in its many manifestations. And somehow, there is nothing so comforting as the knowledge that someone else has met with experiences similar to our own.

Romantic Love

$\mathcal{I}$ ne'er was struck before that hour

With love so sudden and so sweet;

Her face it bloomed like a sweet flower

And stole my heart away complete.

John Clare, 1793–1864
English poet

I shall love you

until death do us part

and then we shall be together

for ever and ever.

Dylan Thomas, 1914–1953
Welsh poet

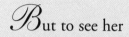

$\mathscr{B}$ut to see her

was to love her,

love but her,

and love forever.

Robert Burns, 1759–1796
Scottish poet

*W*ho ever loved
that loved not
at first sight?

Christopher Marlowe, 1564–1593
English poet, playwright

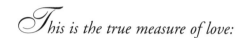

his is the true measure of love:

when we believe that we alone can love,

that no one could ever have loved so before us,

and that no one will ever love in

the same way after us.

Johann von Goethe, 1749–1832
German poet, writer, scientist

$\mathcal{L}$ove is an act

of endless forgiveness,

a tender look

which becomes a habit.

Peter Ustinov, 1921–2004
British actor, director, writer

*G*ive your hearts but not into each other's keeping.

For only the hand of Life can contain your heart.

And stand together yet not too near together.

For the pillars of the temple stand apart,

and the oak tree and the cypress

grow not in each other's shadow.

Kahlil Gibran, 1883–1931
Lebanese poet, artist, mystic

*C*ome live with me and be my Love,

And we will all the pleasures prove

That hills and valleys, dales and fields,

Or woods or sleepy mountain yields.

Christopher Marlowe, 1564–1593
English dramatist, poet

Grow old along with me!

The best is yet to be,

The last of life, for which the first was made:

Our times are in his hand

Who saith, 'A whole I planned,

Youth shows but half, trust God: see all,

Be not afraid!'

Robert Browning, 1812–1889
English poet

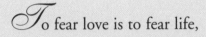

To fear love is to fear life,

and those who fear life

are already three parts dead.

Bertrand Russell, 1872–1970
English philosopher, mathematician, writer

'*T*is better to have loved and lost

Than never to have loved at all.

Lord Alfred Tennyson, 1809–1892
English poet

To be brave is to love someone unconditionally without expecting anything in return. To just give — that takes courage because we don't want to fall flat on our faces or leave ourselves open to hurt.

Madonna, b. 1958
American singer

$\mathscr{T}$he story of love is not important –

what is important is

that one is capable of love.

It is perhaps the only glimpse we are

permitted of eternity.

Helen Hayes, 1900–1993
American actress

Love is a symbol of eternity.

It wipes out all sense of time,

destroying all memory of a beginning

and all fear of an end.

Madame de Stael, 1766–1817
French writer

*The moment you have in your heart
this extraordinary thing called love and feel the depth,
delight, the ecstasy of it, you will discover
that for you the world is transformed.*

Jiddu Krishnamurti, 1895–1986
Indian-born speaker, motivator

*D*rink to me only with thine eyes,

And I will pledge with mine;

Or leave a kiss but in the cup,

And I'll not look for wine.

Ben Jonson, 1572–1637
English dramatist, poet

Tho' small the pledge yet may it be

Remembrance of my love to thee,

And may thy love delight my breast,

Possessing all of thee possest.

Victorian valentine inscription

When you have loved as she has loved,

you grow old beautifully.

W. Somerset Maugham, 1874–1965
English writer, dramatist, physician

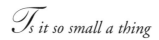

Is it so small a thing

To have enjoyed the sun,

To have lived in the spring,

To have loved, to have thought, to have done?

Matthew Arnold, 1822–1888
English poet

*L*ove those that love you.

Voltaire, 1694–1778
French poet

*Y*ou are always new.

The last of your kisses

Was ever the sweetest.

———————————

John Keats, 1795–1821
English poet

$\mathcal{I}$t is by loving and not by being loved

that one can come nearest the soul of another;

yea where two love it is the loving of each other,

and not the being loved by each other,

that originates and perfects and ensures

their blessedness.

George MacDonald, 1824–1905
Scottish author, poet

*K*eep love in your heart.
A life without it is like a sunless garden
when the flowers are dead.
The consciousness of loving and being loved
brings a warmth and richness to life
that nothing else can bring.

Oscar Wilde, 1854–1900
Irish dramatist, novelist, wit

*L*et him kiss me

with the kisses of his mouth:

For thy love is better than wine.

Song of Solomon, 1:2

Love seeketh not itself to please

Nor for itself hath any care

But for another gives its ease

And builds a Heaven in

Hell's despair.

William Blake, 1757–1827
English poet

*F*or it was not into my ear you whispered

but into my heart.

It was not my lips you kissed

but my soul.

Judy Garland, 1922–1969
American singer, actress

What is love? 'Tis not hereafter;

Present mirth hath present laughter;

What's to come is still unsure:

In delay, there lies not plenty;

Then, come kiss me, sweet and twenty,

Youth's a stuff will not endure.

William Shakespeare, 1564–1616
English dramatist, poet

$\mathcal{L}$ove gives naught but itself
and takes naught but from itself.
Love possesses not
nor would it be possessed;
for love is sufficient unto love.

Khalil Gibran, 1883–1931
Lebanese poet, artist, mystic

My heart is like a singing bird

 Whose nest is in a watered shoot;

My heart is like an apple tree

 Whose boughs are bent with thickest fruit;

My heart is like a rainbow shell

 That paddles in a halcyon sea;

My heart is gladder than all these

 Because my love is come to me.

Christina Rossetti, 1830–1894

English poet

*D*oubt thou the stars are fire;

Doubt that the sun doth move;

Doubt truth to be a liar;

But never doubt I love.

William Shakespeare, 1564–1616
English dramatist, poet

We love being in love;

that's the truth on't.

William Makepeace Thackeray, 1811–1863
English novelist

I cannot fix on the hour,
or the spot, or the look, or the words,
which laid the foundation. It is too long ago.
I was in the middle before I knew I had begun.

Jane Austen, 1775–1817
English novelist

$\mathcal{L}$ove, as is told by the seers of old,

Comes as a butterfly tipped with gold,

Flutters and flies in sunlit skies,

Weaving 'round hearts that were one time cold.

Algernon Swinburne, 1837–1909
English poet

*S*trange how the heart will leap

To see one face at the door,

To hear one voice ring floating out,

One step upon the floor!

Mary Gilmore, 1865–1962
Australian poet, journalist

Love consists in this, that two solitudes

protect and touch and greet each other.

Rainer Maria Rilke, 1875–1926
Swiss-born German poet

Time is

Too slow for those who wait,

Too swift for those who fear,

Too long for those who grieve,

Too short for those who rejoice,

But for those who love, time is Eternity.

Hours fly; flowers die;

New days, new ways, pass by.

Love stays.

Henry van Dyke, 1852–1933
American author, educator

*A*ll, everything that I understand,
I understand only because I love.

Leo Tolstoy, 1828–1910
Russian novelist

O my Luve's like a red, red rose

That's newly sprung in June;

O my Luve's like the melodie

That's sweetly played in tune.

Robert Burns, 1759–1796
Scottish poet

All love at first, like generous wine,

    Ferments and frets until 'tis fine;

But when 'tis settled on the lee,

    And from th'impurer matter free,

Becomes the richer still the older,

    And proves the pleasanter the colder.

Samuel Butler, 1835–1902
English writer

The Power of Love

*T*reasure the love that you receive above all.

It will survive long after your gold

and good health have vanished.

Og Mandino, 1923–1996
American author

The only thing I know about love

is that love is all there is ….

Love can do all but raise the dead.

Emily Dickinson, 1830–1886
American poet

*O*ne word frees us

of all the weight and pain of life;

that word is *love*.

Sophocles, 496–406 BC
Greek tragedian

$\mathcal{L}$ove is a fruit in season at all times
and within the reach of every hand. Anyone
may gather it and no limit is set. Everyone can
reach this love through meditation, spirit of
prayer, and sacrifice by an intense inner life.

Mother Teresa of Calcutta, 1910–1997
Albanian-born missionary

*T*he affirmation of one's own life,

happiness, growth, freedom

is rooted in one's capacity to love.

Erich Fromm, 1900–1980
German-born American psychologist

L ove is the only force capable of transforming an enemy into a friend.

Martin Luther King, Jr., 1929–1968
American civil rights activist, minister

Above all, love each other deeply

because love covers a multitude of sins.

Peter 4: 8

*S*pread love everywhere you go:

first of all in your own home.

Give love to your children,

to your wife or husband,

to a next-door neighbor.

Let no one ever come to you

without leaving better and happier.

Mother Teresa of Calcutta, 1910–1997
Albanian-born missionary

You will find

as you look back upon your life

that the moments when you have truly lived

are the moments when you have done things

in the spirit of love.

Henry Drummond, 1851–1897
Scottish Evangelical writer

$\mathscr{A}$ loving heart is the truest wisdom.

Charles Dickens, 1812–1870
English writer

*A*ll love is sweet,

Given or returned.

Common as light is love,

And its familiar voice wearies not ever.

Percy Bysshe Shelley, 1792–1822
English poet

If, from time to time,

we look at the blessings in our lives,

at the warmth and care and love so many people

respond with when there is a tragedy,

at the fact that we can walk and talk

and eat and breathe, then maybe we would …

become aware that all negative thoughts

bring with them are more negativity,

but love shared returns a thousandfold.

Elisabeth Kübler-Ross, 1926–2004
Swiss-born American psychiatrist

Mercy is Love being gracious.

Eloquence is Love talking.

Prophecy is Love foretelling.

Faith is Love believing.

Charity is Love acting.

Sacrifice is Love offering itself.

Patience is Love waiting.

Endurance is Love abiding.

Hope is Love expecting.

Peace is Love resting.

Prayer is Love communing.

Unknown

Love comforteth like sunshine after rain.

William Shakespeare, 1564–1616
English playwright, poet

*L*ove alone

is capable of uniting human beings

in such a way as to complete and fulfill them

for it alone takes them and joins them

by what is deepest in themselves.

Pierre Teilhard de Chardin, 1881–1955
French Jesuit priest

$\mathcal{L}$ove will teach us all things.

But we must learn how to win love;

it's got with difficulty.

It is a possession dearly bought

with much labor and a long time.

For one must love not sometimes,

for a passing moment,

but always.

Feodor Dostoevsky, 1821–1881
Russian novelist

$\mathcal{T}$o love means never to be afraid

of the windstorms of life; should you shield the

canyons from the windstorms, you would

never see the true beauty of their carvings.

Elisabeth Kübler-Ross, 1926–2004
Swiss-born American psychiatrist

*O*nly love can be divided endlessly

and still not diminish.

Anne Morrow Lindbergh, 1906–2001
American aviator, writer

Great is the power of might and mind,

But only love can make us kind,

And all we are or hope to be

Is empty pride and vanity —

If love is not a part of all,

The greatest man is very small.

Helen Steiner Rice, 1900–1981
American poet

*To love deeply in one direction
makes us more loving in all others.*

Anne-Sophie Swetchine
Russian author

$\mathcal{B}$eing deeply loved by someone

gives you strength;

loving someone deeply

gives you courage.

Lao Tze, c. 6 BC
Chinese philosopher

Love is patient;

   love is kind;

it does not envy;

   it does not boast;

it is not proud;

   it is not rude;

it is not self-seeking;

   it is not easily angered;

it keeps no records of wrongs.

Corinthians 13: 4–5

The root of the matter is a very simple and old-fashioned thing, a thing so simple that I am almost ashamed to mention it for fear of the derisive smile with which wise cynics will greet my words. The thing I mean — please forgive me for mentioning it — is love, or compassion. If you feel this, you have a motive for existence, a guide to action, a reason for courage, an imperative necessity for intellectual honesty.

Bertrand Russell, 1872–1970
English philosopher, mathematician, writer

I define love thus:

the will to extend oneself

for the purpose of nurturing one's own

or another's spiritual growth.

M. Scott Peck, b. 1936
American psychiatrist, writer

$\mathcal{I}$n our life, there is a single color,

as on an artist's palette, which provides

the meaning of life and art.

It is the color of love.

Marc Chagall, 1887–1985
French painter

*A*ge does not protect you from love.

But love, to some extent,

protects you from age.

Jeanne Moreau, b. 1928
French actress

*L*ove makes all hard hearts gentle.

George Herbert, 1593–1633
English poet

$\mathcal{I}$f we make our goal to live a life

of compassion and unconditional love,

then the world will indeed become

a garden where all kinds of flowers

can bloom and grow.

Elisabeth Kübler-Ross, 1926–2004
Swiss-born American psychiatrist

*L*ove has nothing to do
with what you are expecting to get –
only what you are expecting to give.

Katharine Hepburn, 1907–2003
American actress

The Comfort of Friendship

Oh, the inexpressible comfort

of feeling safe with a person:

having neither to weigh thoughts

nor measure words,

but pour them all out, as they are,

chaff and grain together, knowing that

a faithful hand will take and sift them,

keep what is worth keeping, and then,

with the breath of kindness,

blow the rest away.

George Eliot, 1819–1880
English novelist

$\mathcal{F}$riendship improves happiness

and abates misery

by doubling our joy

and dividing our grief.

Joseph Addison, 1672–1719
English essayist

$\mathscr{F}$rom quiet home and first beginning,

Out to the undiscovered ends,

There's nothing worth the wear of winning,

But laughter and the love of friends.

Hilaire Belloc, 1870–1953
English writer

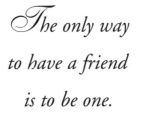

The only way

to have a friend

is to be one.

Ralph Waldo Emerson, 1803–1882
American poet, essayist, teacher

If someone listens

or stretches out a hand

or whispers a word of encouragement

or attempts to understand a lonely person,

extraordinary things begin to happen.

Loretta Firzaris, b. 1920
American educator, writer

Whoever knows

how to return a kindness he has received

must be a friend above price.

Sophocles, 496–406 BC
Greek tragedian

The best portion of a good man's life:

His little, nameless, unremembered acts

Of kindness and love.

William Wordsworth, 1770–1850
English poet

By compassion,

we make other's misery our own,

and so, by relieving them,

we also relieve ourselves.

Thomas Browne, 1605–1682
English author, physician

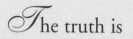

The truth is

friendship is every bit

as sacred and eternal

as marriage.

Katherine Mansfield, 1888–1923
New Zealand short story writer

A friend

is one who knows you

and loves you just the same.

Elbert Hubbard, 1856–1915
American editor, writer

Others have their family,
but to a solitary and an exile,
his friends are everything.

Willa Cather, 1873–1947
American writer

I get by

with a little help

from my friends.

John Lennon, 1940–1980
English singer, songwriter, guitarist

If I can stop one heart from breaking,

I shall not live in vain;

If I can ease one life the aching

Or cool one pain

Or help one fainting robin

Unto his nest again,

I shall not live in vain.

Emily Dickinson, 1830–1886
American poet

It is a wonderful advantage to a man,

in every pursuit of avocation,

to secure an adviser in a sensible woman....

A man's best female friend

is a wife of good sense and good heart

who loves him.

Edward Bulwer-Lytton, 1803–1873
English novelist, dramatist, politician

$\mathcal{T}$hink where man's glory

Most begins and ends

And say that my glory

Was I had such friends.

W. B. Yeats, 1865–1939
Irish poet, dramatist, writer

Let there be no purpose in friendship

save the deepening of the spirit.

For love that seeks aught

but the disclosure of its own mystery

is not love but a net cast forth,

and only the unprofitable is caught.

Kahlil Gibran, 1883–1931
Lebanese poet, artist, mystic

*L*ove is like the wild rose-briar,

Friendship like the holly tree.

The holly is dark when the rose-briar blooms,

But which one blooms most constantly?

Emily Brontë, 1818–1848
English novelist, poet

It's the friends

you can call up at 4 a.m.

that matter.

Marlene Dietrich, 1901–1992
German-born actress

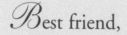

$\mathcal{B}$est friend,

my well-spring in the wilderness!

George Eliot, 1819–1880
English novelist

A real friend

is one who walks in

when the rest of the world walks out.

Walter Winchell, 1879–1972
American journalist

$\mathcal{A}$ friend should bear

his friend's infirmities....

William Shakespeare, 1564–1616
English dramatist, poet

When we can honestly ask ourselves

which person in our lives means most to us,

we often find that it is those who,

instead of giving advice, solutions, or cures,

have chosen rather to share our pain

and touch our wounds

with a warm and tender hand.

Heni Nouwen, 1932–1996
Dutch-born priest, writer

$\mathcal{L}$ife is to be fortified by many friendships.

To love and be loved

is the greatest happiness of existence.

Sydney Smith, 1771–1845
English clergyman, essayist, wit

$\mathcal{W}$hat do we live for,

if it is not to make life

less difficult for each other?

George Eliot, 1819–1880
English novelist

$\mathcal{Y}$our friend is your needs answered.

He is your field which you sow with love

and reap with thanksgiving.

And he is your board and your fireside.

For you come to him with your hunger,

and you seek him for peace.

Kahlil Gibran, 1883–1931
Lebanese poet, artist, mystic

Can I see another's woe
And not be in sorrow too?
Can I see another's grief
And not seek for kind relief?

William Blake, 1757–1827
English poet, artist

*L*ots of people want to ride in the limo,

but what you want is someone

who will take the bus with you

when the limo breaks down.

Oprah Winfrey, b.1954
American television personality

The glory of friendship
is not the outstretched hand
nor the kindly smile
nor the joy of companionship;
it is the spiritual inspiration
that comes to one
when he discovers that
someone else believes in him
and is willing to trust him.

Ralph Waldo Emerson, 1803–1882
American poet, essayist, teacher

$\mathcal{A}$ person who seeks help for a friend,

while in need himself,

will be answered first.

The Talmud

We All Stumble

$\mathcal{A}$nd remember,

we all stumble,

every one of us.

That's why it's a comfort

to go hand in hand.

Emily Kimbrough, 1899–1989
American writer

The greatest glory
is not in never falling
but in rising
every time we fall.

Confucius, c. 55–478 BC
Chinese philosopher

Only those who dare to fail greatly

can ever achieve greatly.

Robert F. Kennedy, 1925–1968
American senator, attorney-general

ou know,

by the time you've reached my age,

you've made plenty of mistakes

if you've lived your life properly.

Ronald Reagan, 1911–2004
President of the United States of America

*E*xpect trouble as an inevitable part of life,

and when it comes,

hold your head high,

look it squarely in the eye, and say,

'I will be bigger than you. You cannot defeat me.'

Then, repeat to yourself

the most comforting words of all,

'This too will pass.'

Ann Landers, 1918–2002
American journalist

I think these difficult times

have helped me to understand

better than before

how infinitely rich and

beautiful life is in every way

and that so many things

that one goes around worrying about

are of no importance whatsoever.

Isak Dinesen, 1885–1962
Danish writer

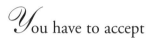ou have to accept

whatever comes along,

and the only important thing is

that you meet it

with the best you have to give.

Eleanor Roosevelt, 1884–1962
First Lady of the United States of America

*M*ake it a rule of life

never to regret and never look back.

We all live in suspense,

from day to day,

from hour to hour....

Mary McCarthy, 1912–1989
American author, critic

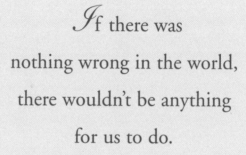

*I*f there was
nothing wrong in the world,
there wouldn't be anything
for us to do.

George Bernard Shaw, 1856–1950
Irish dramatist, writer, critic

*W*henever I have found that I have blundered

or that my work has been imperfect,

and when I have been contemptuously criticized

and even when I have been overpraised

so that I have felt mortified,

it has been my greatest comfort

to say hundreds of times to myself that

'I have worked as hard and as well as I could,

and no man can do more than this.'

Charles Darwin, 1809–1882
British scientist

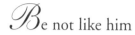

Be not like him

who sits by his fireside

and watches the fire go out,

then blows vainly upon the dead ashes.

Do not give up hope

or yield to despair

because of that which is past,

for to bewail the irretrievable is the worst

of human frailties.

Kahlil Gibran, 1883–1931
Lebanese poet, artist, mystic

*M*ake the most of your regrets....

To regret deeply is to live afresh.

Henry David Thoreau, 1817–1862
American essayist, poet

My downfall

raises me to great heights.

Napoleon Bonaparte, 1769–1821
French emperor, general

To regret one's own experiences

is to arrest one's own development.

To deny one's own experiences is to

put a lie into the lips of one's own life.

It is no less than a denial of the soul.

Oscar Wilde, 1854–1900
Irish dramatist, novelist, wit

*P*roblems call forth

our courage and our wisdom;

indeed they create

our courage and our wisdom.

It is only because of problems

that we grow mentally and spiritually.

It is through the pain of confronting

and resolving problems

that we learn.

M. Scott Peck, b. 1936
American psychiatrist, writer

Nobody makes a greater mistake

than he who does nothing

because he could do so little.

Edmund Burke, 1729–1797
British politician

*E*ven at the worst,

there is always a way out,

a hidden secret

that can turn failure into success

and despair into happiness.

No situation is so dark

that there is not a ray of light.

Norman Vincent Peale, 1898–1993
American writer, minister

$\mathscr{A}$nyone can carry his burden, however hard,

until nightfall.

Anyone can do his work, however hard,

for one day.

Anyone can live sweetly, patiently, lovingly, purely

till the sun goes down.

And this is all life really means.

Robert Louis Stevenson, 1850–1894
Scottish writer, poet, essayist

*R*egret is an appalling waste of energy;

you can't build on it;

it is good only for wallowing in.

Katherine Mansfield, 1888–1923
New Zealand short story writer

There's no point in dwelling

on what might or could have been.

You just have to go forward.

Jack Nicholson, b. 1937
American actor

What's gone and what's past help

Should be past grief.

William Shakespeare, 1564–1616
English playwright, poet

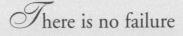

$\mathcal{T}$here is no failure

except in not trying.

Elbert Hubbard, 1856–1915
American editor, writer

$\mathcal{E}$ven a mistake

may turn out to be

the one thing necessary

to a worthwhile achievement.

Henry Ford, 1863–1947
American car manufacturer

$\mathcal{T}$he marvelous richness of human experience

would lose something of rewarding joy

if there were no limitations to overcome.

The hilltop hour would not be so half wonderful

if there were no dark valleys to traverse.

Helen Keller, 1880–1968
American writer, scholar

$\mathscr{A}$ll things are difficult

before they are easy.

Thomas Fuller, 1608–1661
English cleric, historian

*N*othing would be done at all

if a man waited

until he could do it so well

that no one could find fault with it.

Cardinal Newman, 1801–1890
English theologian

Adversity

has the same effect on a man that

severe training has on the pugilist —

it reduces him to his fighting weight.

Josh Billings, 1818–1885
American humorist

Character consists of what you do

on the third and fourth tries.

James A. Michener, 1907–1997
American writer

A man of character
finds a special attractiveness in difficulty,
since it is only by
coming to grips with difficulty
that he can realize his potentialities.

Charles de Gaulle, 1890–1970
French statesman, general

The hill, though high, I covet to ascend;

The difficulty will not offend,

For I perceive the way to life lies here.

Come, pluck up heart, let's neither faint nor fear;

Better, though difficult, the right way to go,

Than wrong, though easy,

Where the end is woe.

John Bunyan, 1628–1688
English writer, moralist

*L*ife affords no higher pleasure

than that of surmounting difficulties,

passing from one step of success to another,

forming new wishes and

seeing them gratified.

Samuel Johnson, 1709–1784
English lexicographer, critic, essayist

$\mathcal{T}$hose things that hurt instruct.

Benjamin Franklin, 1705–1790
American statesman, scientist

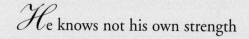

$\mathcal{H}$e knows not his own strength

that hath not met adversity.

Ben Jonson, 1573–1637
English dramatist

I could do nothing without my problems;

they toughen my mind.

In fact, I tell my assistants

not to bring me their successes

for they weaken me,

but rather to bring me their problems,

for they strengthen me.

Charles Franklin Kettering, 1876–1958
American engineer, inventor

Do what is easy

as if it were difficult

and what is difficult

as if it were easy.

Baltasar Gracian, 1601–1658
Spanish priest

Be a Friend to Yourself

*M*y friend,

my companion, held most dear,

my soul,

my other self, my inward friend.

Mary Sidney Herbert, 1561–1621
English writer, poet

I have to live with myself, and so

   I want to be fit for myself to know,

I want to be able as days go by,

   Always to look myself straight in the eye.

Edgar A. Guest, 1881–1959
English-born American poet, writer

*T*here is nobody else like you.

The more you can quiet your own thoughts,

fears, doubts, and suspicions,

the more will be revealed to you

from the higher realms of imagination,

intuition, and inspiration.

Kenneth Wydro, b. 1933
American lecturer

Every individual human being

born on this earth

has the capacity to become

a unique and special person,

unlike any who has ever existed before

or will ever exist again.

Elisabeth Kübler-Ross, 1926–2004
American psychiatrist, writer

*A*ccept yourself as you are.

Otherwise you will never see opportunity.

You will not feel free to move toward it;

you will feel you are not deserving.

Maxwell Maltz, 1899–1975
American surgeon, motivational writer

$\mathcal{R}$esolve to be thyself; and know that he

Who finds himself, loses his misery.

Matthew Arnold, 1822–1888
English poet, critic, essayist

Care no more for the opinions of others,

for those voices. Do the hardest thing on earth for you.

Act for yourself. Face the truth.

Katherine Mansfield, 1888–1923
New Zealand short story writer

$\mathcal{I}$ was raised to sense

what someone else wanted me to be....

It took me a long time not to judge myself

through someone else's eyes.

Sally Field, b. 1946
American actor

$\mathcal{B}$ecome friends with yourself;

learn to appreciate who you are

and your unique gifts.

Be patient with yourself

and use your sense of humor

to keep things in perspective.

Dorothy Edgerton, b. 1911
American writer

In everyone, there is something precious
found in no one else;
so honor each man
for what is hidden within him —
for what he has
and none of his fellows.

Hasidic saying

*F*riendship with oneself is all-important

because without it one cannot be friends

with anyone else in the world.

Eleanor Roosevelt, 1884–1962
First Lady of the United States of America

Start treating yourself as if

you're the most important asset

you'll ever have.

After all, aren't you?

Anonymous

Our problem is that we make the mistake

of comparing ourselves with other people.

You are not inferior or superior

to any human being....

You do not determine your success

by comparing yourself to others;

rather you determine your success

by comparing your accomplishments

to your capabilities.

You are 'number one' when you do the best you can

with what you have, every day.

Zig Ziglar, b. 1926
American motivational writer

*O*ne should treat oneself

as one does one's friends – critically

but with affection.

Frances Partridge, 1900–2004
English diarist

*N*othing is a greater impediment
to being on good terms with others
than being ill at ease with oneself.

Honoré de Balzac, 1799–1850
French writer

One must have

the adventurous daring

to accept oneself

as a bundle of possibilities

and undertake the most

interesting game in the world:

making the most of one's best.

Harry Emerson Fosdick, 1878–1969
American theologian, author

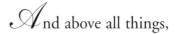nd above all things,

never think that you're not good enough yourself.

A man should never think that.

My belief is that

in life people will take you

at your own reckoning.

Anthony Trollope, 1815–1882
British novelist

Loss and Comfort

Master, what is the best way to meet

the loss of someone we love?

By knowing that when we truly love, it is never lost.

It is only after death that the depth of the bond

is truly felt, and our loved one becomes more a part

of us than was possible in life.

———————

Oriental tradition

$\mathcal{T}$here is a land of the living

and a land of the dead,

and the bridge is love.

Thornton Wilder, 1897–1975
American author, dramatist

Ever has it been

that love knows not its own depth

until the hour of separation.

Kahlil Gibran, 1883–1931
Lebanese poet, artist, mystic

$\mathcal{U}$nable are the Loved to die

For Love is Immortality,

Nay, it is Deity –

Unable they that love to die

For Love reforms Vitality

Into Divinity.

Emily Dickinson, 1830–1886
American poet

When you pass through deep waters,

I will be with you;

your troubles will not overwhelm you.

Isiah 43:2

*H*ave courage for the greatest sorrows of life

and patience for the small ones,

and when you have laboriously

accomplished your daily tasks,

go to sleep in peace.

God is awake.

Victor Hugo, 1802–1885
French poet, writer

There is a sacredness in tears
They are not the mark of weakness
but of power.
They speak more eloquently
than ten thousand tongues.
They are messengers of overwhelming grief,
of deep contrition,
and of unspeakable love.

Henry Irving, 1838–1905
English stage actor

*T*he knowledge that another

has felt as we have felt,

and seen things not much otherwise

than we have seen them,

will continue to the end to be

one of life's choicest blessings.

Robert Louis Stevenson, 1850–1894
Scottish writer, poet, essayist

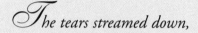

The tears streamed down,

and I let them flow

as freely as they would,

making of them

a pillow for my heart.

St. Augustine, 354–430 AD
Roman Catholic saint

The tears you shed are purer than

the laughter of him that seeks to forget

and sweeter than the mockery of the scoffer.

These tears cleanse the heart

of the blight of hatred

and teach man to share the pain

of the broken-hearted.

They are the tears of Nazarene.

Kahlil Gibran, 1883–1931
Lebanese poet, artist, mystic

*I*n the night of death,
hope sees a star, and listening
love can hear the rustle of a wing.

Robert Green Ingersoll, 1833–1899
American lawyer, soldier, writer

Truly, it is in the darkness

that one finds the light,

so when we are in sorrow,

then this light is nearest to us.

Johannes Eckhart, c. 1260–1327
German mystic

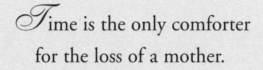

Time is the only comforter
for the loss of a mother.

Jane Welsh Carlyle, 1801–1866
English writer

*M*ake yourself nests of pleasant thoughts.

None of us yet know,

for none of us has been taught in early youth,

what fairy palaces we may build of

beautiful thoughts – proof against all adversity.

Bright fancies, satisfied memories,

noble histories, faithful sayings,

treasure-houses of precious and restful thoughts,

which care cannot disturb, nor pain make gloomy,

nor poverty take away from us –

houses built without hands,

for our souls to live in.

John Ruskin, 1819–1900
English author, poet

She is roses and London gardens;

she is wartime movies

and Frank Sinatra songs;

she is Italy and France and China tea.

She is soaked through everything I see.

I look at my face in the mirror,

at my mannerisms, the veins in my hands,

and realize she will always be with me.

Harriet Walter, b. 1950
English actor

*B*ereavement is the deepest initiation
into the mysteries of human life.

W. R. Inge, 1860–1954
English author

To Lady Raleigh on the death of their son

I was loath to write because I knew not how to comfort you;

and God knows, I never knew what sorrow meant

till now ....

Sir Walter Raleigh, 1552–1618
English courtier, explorer, poet, historian

I did not get over the loss of my loved ones;

rather, I absorbed the loss into my life,

like soil receives decaying matter,

until it became a part of who I am.

Sorrow took up

permanent residence in my soul

and enlarged it.

Gerald Sittser, b. 1950
American philosopher

*W*e are healed of a suffering

only by experiencing it to the full.

Marcel Proust, 1871–1922
French writer

For everything, there is a season

and a time for every matter under heaven:

a time to be born

and a time to die....

a time to weep

and a time to laugh....

Ecclesiastes 3:1 –2, 4

This is the hour of lead

Remembered if outlived

As freezing persons

Recollect

The snow –

First chill, then stupor, then

The letting go.

Emily Dickinson, 1830–1886
American poet

The sorrow for the dead is
the only sorrow from which
we refuse to be divorced....
the love which survives the tomb
is one of the noblest attributes
of the soul.

Washington Irving, 1783–1859
American writer

$\mathcal{G}$rief is a most peculiar thing.

We're so helpless in the face of it.

It's like a window that opens of its own accord,

letting in a cold draught.

There's nothing we can do but shiver.

But it opens a little less each time,

and one day we wonder

what has become of the chill.

———

Unknown

No one can tell you
when the grieving time is up
because it is different for everybody.
Only you know when you can
take a step back into the world
and for how long.

Edwin Maher, b. 1941
Australian TV weather reporter, writer

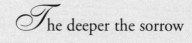

The deeper the sorrow

that carves into your being,

the more joy you can contain.

Joy and sorrow are inseparable.

Kahlil Gibran, 1883–1931
Lebanese poet, artist, mystic

*W*here there is sorrow

there is holy ground.

Oscar Wilde, 1854–1900
Irish dramatist, novelist, wit

*H*appiness is beneficial for the body,

but it is grief that develops

the powers of the mind.

Marcel Proust, 1871–1922
French writer

I do not believe that sheer suffering teaches.

If suffering alone taught,

all the world would be wise

since everyone suffers.

To suffering must be added mourning,

understanding, patience, love, openness,

and the willingness

to remain vulnerable.

Anne Morrow Lindbergh, 1906–2001
American pilot, poet, writer

'*The mountains and hills may crumble,*

but my love for you will never end;

I will keep forever my promise of peace.'

So says the Lord who loves you.

Isaiah 54: 10

*P*eace comes within the souls of men

when they realize their relationship, their oneness,

with the universe and all its powers....

_____
Native American tradition

The heart's affections are divided

like the branches of the cedar tree;

if the tree loses one branch,

it will suffer, but it does not die.

It will pour all its vitality into the next branch

so that it will grow and fill

the empty space.

Kahlil Gibran, 1883–1931
Lebanese poet, artist, mystic

Sorrow comes in great waves...

but it rolls over us,

and though it may almost smother us,

it leaves us on the spot,

and we know that if it is strong,

we are stronger inasmuch as it passes

and we remain.

Henry James, 1843–1916
American writer

*A*lthough the world is full of suffering,

it is also full of the overcoming of it.

Helen Keller, 1880–1968
American author, lecturer

$\mathcal{G}$rief drives men
into habits of serious reflection,
sharpens the understanding,
and softens the heart.

John Adams, 1735–1826
President of the United States of America

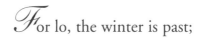For lo, the winter is past;

the rain is over and gone; the flowers appear on the earth;

the time of the singing of birds is come; and the voice of the

turtle is heard in our land.

The Song of Solomon 2: 11–12

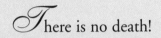

There is no death!

What seems so is transition;

This life of mortal breath

Is but a suburb of the life Elysian,

Whose portal we call death.

Henry Wadsworth Longfellow, 1807–1882
American poet

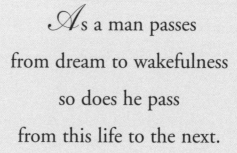

$\mathcal{A}$s a man passes

from dream to wakefulness

so does he pass

from this life to the next.

———————

Hindu tradition

$\mathcal{I}$t is impossible that anything so natural,

so necessary, and so universal as death

should ever have been designed by providence

as an evil to mankind.

Jonathan Swift, 1667–1745
Irish satirist, poet, essayist, cleric

*T*he world is the land of the dying;

the next is the land of the living.

Tyron Edwards, 1809–1894
American theologian

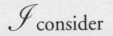consider

that what we suffer at this present time

cannot be compared at all

with the glory that is

going to be revealed to us.

———

Romans 8:18

$\mathcal{E}$arth has no sorrow

that heaven cannot heal.

Sir Thomas More, 1478–1535
English writer, politician

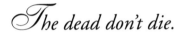

The dead don't die.

They look on and help.

D. H. Lawrence, 1855–1930
English writer, poet

What is this world?

A dream within a dream – as we grow older,

each step is an awakening.

The grave the last step? No – it is

the last and final awakening.

Sir Walter Scott, 1771–1832
Scottish novelist, poet

You would know the secret of death.

But how shall you find it

unless you seek it in the heart of life?

The owl whose night-bound eyes

are blind unto the day

cannot unveil the mystery of light.

If you would indeed behold the spirit of death,

open your heart wide unto the body of life.

For life and death are one,

even as river and sea are one.

Kahlil Gibran, 1883–1931
Lebanese poet, artist, mystic

What is our death but a night's sleep?

For as through sleep

all weariness and faintness pass away and cease

and the powers of the spirit come back again

so that in the morning we arise fresh

and strong and joyous;

so at the last day, we shall rise again

as if we had only slept a night

and shall be fresh and strong.

Martin Luther, 1483–1546
German theologian

We sometimes congratulate ourselves

at the moment of waking

from a troubled dream;

it may be so the moment after death.

Nathaniel Hawthorne, 1804–1864
American writer

*L*ife is a great surprise.

I do not see why death should not be

an even greater one.

Vladimir Nabokov, 1899–1977
Russian writer

The Wealth Within

$\mathcal{L}$earn to get in touch
with the silence within yourself
and know that everything in this life
has a purpose.

Elisabeth Kübler-Ross, b. 1926–2004
Swiss-born American psychiatrist, writer

Within yourself

is a stillness and a sanctuary

to which you can retreat at any time

and be yourself.

Hermann Hesse, 1877–1962
German writer

O Solitude, the soul's best friend,

That man acquainted with himself

Dost make.

Charles Cotton, 1630–1687
English poet

In meditation,

it is possible to dive deeper into the mind

to a place where there is no disturbance

and there is absolute solitude.

It is at this point in the profound stillness

that the sound of the mind can be heard.

A.E.I. Falconar, b. 1926
Indian-born philosopher

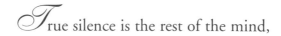

True silence is the rest of the mind,

and it is to the spirit

what sleep is to the body,

nourishment and refreshment.

William Penn, 1644–1718
English-born Quaker, founder of Pennsylvania

Solitude –

walking alone, doing things alone –

is the most blessed thing in the world.

The mind relaxes and thoughts begin to flow,

and I think that I am beginning to

find myself a little.

Helen Hayes, 1900–1993
American actress

It is not necessary

to go off on a tour of great cathedrals

in order to find the Deity.

Look within.

You have to sit still to do it.

Albert Schweitzer, 1875–1965
German theologian, physician

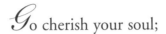

Go cherish your soul;

expel companions;

set your habits to a life of solitude;

then will the faculties

rise fair and full within.

Ralph Waldo Emerson, 1803–1882
American poet, essayist, teacher

In solitude,

one can achieve

a good relationship

with oneself.

May Sarton, 1912–1995
American poet, writer

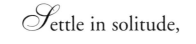

$\mathscr{S}$ettle in solitude,

and you will come upon Him

in yourself.

St. Theresa, 1515–1582
Spanish nun

'Tis not in seeking,
'Tis not in endless striving,
Thy quest is found.
Be still and listen.
Be still, and drink the silence
Of all around.
Not for crying,
Not for loud beseeching
Will peace draw near.
Rest with palms folded;
Rest with thine eyelids fallen –
Lo, peace is here.

Edward Rowland Sill, 1841–1887
American poet

I find there is a quality

to being alone

that is incredibly precious.

Life rushes back into the void,

richer, more vivid,

fuller than before.

Anne Morrow Lindbergh, 1906–2001
American aviator, writer

*W*hat angel

in my own remote childhood

taught me when alone to be happy?

What gratitude

could repay such a boon?

Walter De La Mare, 1873–1956
English poet, writer

*Genuine tranquillity of the heart
and perfect peace of mind,
the highest blessings on earth after health,
are to be found only in solitude and,
as a permanent disposition,
only in the deepest seclusion.*

Arthur Schopenhauer, 1788–1860
German philosopher

When I begin to sit

with the dawn in solitude,

I begin to really live.

It makes me treasure

every single moment of life.

Gloria Vanderbilt, 1924–1997
American actress, fashion designer

$\mathcal{L}$iving in solitude

till the fullness of time,

I still kept the dew of my youth

and the freshness of my heart.

Nathaniel Hawthorne, 1804–1864
American novelist, short story writer

$\mathcal{W}$e need to find God,

and He cannot be found in noise and restlessness.

God is the friend of silence....

The more we receive in silent prayer,

the more we can give in our active life.

We need silence to be able to touch souls.

Mother Teresa of Calcutta, 1910–1997
Albanian-born missionary

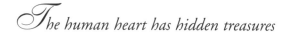

The human heart has hidden treasures

in secret kept, in silence sealed.

Charlotte Brontë, 1816–1855
English writer

*T*ruth is within ourselves; it take no rise

From outward things, what'er you may believe.

There is an inmost center in us all

Where truth abides in fullness.

Robert Browning, 1812–1889
English poet, playwright

In the attitude of silence,

the soul finds the path in a clearer light,

and what is elusive and deceptive

resolves itself into crystal clearness.

Mahatma Gandhi, 1869–1948
Indian political philosopher

O golden Silence, bid our souls be still,

And on the foolish fretting of our care,

Lay thy soft touch of healing unaware.

Julia Dorr, 1825–1913
American poet

The goal of a healthy solitude is love:

love and acceptance of ourselves

as we are and where we are

and love and compassion for others.

Dorothy Payne, 1887–1968
American philanthropist, social activist

So it is

that every spiritual healing is the result

of one individual sitting in the Silence,

quietly, peacefully waiting,

and the Spirit comes through

the consciousness of that one –

the voice thunders in the Silence,

and the Earth melts.

Joel S. Goldsmith, 1892–1964
American motivational writer

What a lovely surprise

to finally discover how unlonely

being alone can be.

Ellen Burstyn, b. 1932
American actress

*T*each us to care and not to care.

Teach us to sit still.

T. S. Eliot, 1888–1965
American-born British poet

$\mathcal{M}$y home is my retreat

and resting place from the wars.

I try to keep this corner as a haven

against the tempest outside

as I do another corner

of my soul.

*Y*our vision will become clear

only when you can look into your heart.

Who looks outside, dreams.

Who looks inside, awakes.

Carl Jung, 1875–1961
Swiss psychiatrist

Prayers and Blessings

Oh Lord, help me

To be calm when things go wrong,

To persevere when things are difficult,

To be helpful to those in need,

And to be sympathetic to those whose

hearts are heavy.

———

Unknown

*L*et nothing disturb you.

Let nothing frighten you.

Everything passes away except God.

St. Theresa, 1515–1582
Spanish nun

Let there be many windows in your soul

That all the glories of the universe

May beautify it.

Ralph Waldo Trine, 1866–1958
American poet, writer

$\mathcal{D}$eep peace of the running wave to you.

Deep peace of the flowing air to you.

Deep peace of the quiet earth to you.

Deep peace of the shining stars to you.

Deep peace of the Son of Peace to you.

_____

Celtic benediction

Teach us delight in simple things,

    And mirth that has no bitter springs,

Forgiveness free of evil done,

    And love to all men 'neath the sun.

Rudyard Kipling, 1865–1936
Indian-born English writer, poet

$\mathcal{G}$rant me, O Lord,

the royalty of inward happiness

and the serenity which comes with living close to Thee.

Daily renew the sense of joy, and let the

eternal spirit of the Father dwell in my soul and body,

filling every corner of my heart with light and grace,

so that bearing about with me the infection of

a good courage, I may be a diffuser of life

and may meet all ills and crosses

with gallant and high-hearted happiness,

giving Thee thanks always for all things.

Robert Louis Stevenson, 1850–1894
Scottish writer, poet

*H*e prayeth well who loveth well

Both man and bird and beast.

He prayeth best who loveth best

All things both great and small;

For the dear God who loveth us,

He made and loveth all.

Samuel Taylor Coleridge, 1772–1834
English poet, philosopher

$\mathcal{P}$rayer is the song of the heart.

It reaches the ear of God even if it is mingled

with the cry and the tumult of a thousand men.

Kahlil Gibran, 1883–1931
Lebanese poet, artist, mystic

O Thou who art at home

Deep in my heart,

Enable me to join you

Deep in my heart.

The Talmud

*T*each me to feel another's woe,

To hide the fault I see;

That mercy I to others show,

That mercy show to me.

Alexander Pope, 1688–1744
English poet

Help me to be

Cheerful when things go wrong;

Persevering when things are difficult;

And serene when things are irritating.

Enable me to be

Helpful to those in difficulties;

Kind to those in need;

Sympathetic to those whose hearts are sad.

―――――

Unknown

$\mathcal{G}$od grant me the serenity

to accept the things

that cannot be changed;

courage to change

the things I can;

and wisdom to know

the difference.

Reinhold Niebuhr, 1892–1971
American theologian

$\mathscr{O}$ Lord,

grant that I may not so much

seek to be consoled as to console;

to be understood as to understand;

to be loved as to love;

for it is in giving that we receive;

it is in pardoning that we are pardoned;

and it is dying

that we are born to Eternal Life.

St. Francis of Assisi, 1181–1226
Founder of Franciscan Order

The peace of God, the peace of men,

   Be upon each window, each door,

Upon each hole that lets in light,

   Upon the four corners of my house,

Upon the four corners of my bed.

_____

Gaelic blessing

God,

help us not to despise or oppose

what we do not understand.

William Penn, 1644–1718
English-born Quaker, founder of Pennsylvania

A single grateful thought

raised to heaven

is the most perfect prayer.

Gotthold Ephraim Lessing, 1729–1781
German writer, philosopher

Pals carry happy hearts,
knowing they are pals for always!